Beliefs & Religions
AROUND THE WORLD

Story by
Judy Kirton

Illustrations by
Val Lawton

Your Nickel's Worth Publishing

For my children & grandchildren
J.K.

In memory of my dad
V.L.

BELIEFS & RELIGIONS AROUND THE WORLD
Story © Judy Kirton, 2011
Illustrations © Val Lawton, 2011

Manufactured by Friesens Corporation in Altona, MB, Canada
April 2011
Job #63790

Library and Archives Canada Cataloguing in Publication

Kirton, Judy, 1947-
Beliefs & religions around the world / Judy Kirton ; illustrations by Val Lawton.

ISBN 978-1-894431-60-6

1. Religions—Juvenile literature. I. Lawton, Val, 1962- II. Title.
III. Title: Beliefs and religions around the world.

BL92.K57 2011   j200   C2011-901393-2

The beliefs and religions in this book appear in the order of their worldwide membership based on current statistical information from "Major Religions of the World Ranked by Adherents." http://www.adherents.com/Religions_By_Adherents.html. p. 32. "The Golden Rule Across the World's Religions." Scarboro Missions, Toronto, ON. 2000. Used with permission.

Design by Heather Nickel
Printed in Canada

Your Nickel's Worth Publishing
Regina, SK.

www.yournickelsworth.com

FSC
www.fsc.org
MIX
Paper from
responsible sources
FSC® C016245

ENVIRONMENTAL BENEFITS STATEMENT
Your Nickel's Worth Publishing saved the following resources by printing the pages of this book on chlorine free paper made with 10% post-consumer waste.

WATER	SOLID WASTE	GREENHOUSE GASES
114 GALLONS	7 POUNDS	24 POUNDS

Calculations based on research by Environmental Defense and the Paper Task Force. Manufactured at Friesens Corporation

Introduction

"You may give them your love but not your thoughts,
for they have their own thoughts."
— KAHLIL GIBRAN, *On Children*—

This little book offers parents, grandparents, teachers and other caregivers who read to young children a simple way of introducing them to what different people believe. It is an important part of what we teach them and is one way to nurture respect and acceptance.

The descriptions inside represent only a small sample of the variety of beliefs, religions and customs around the world, each with its own rich heritage to discover.

Hi! My name is Sarah. My family is **Christian** (KRISS-chun).

Christians live all over the world.

The **Bible** (BY-bull) is our special book.

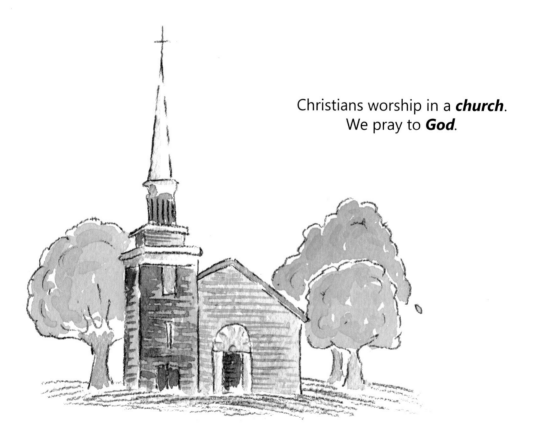

Christians worship in a **church**.
We pray to **God**.

Christmas (KRISS-muss) is a special time of year for us. It is the birthday of **Jesus** (JEE-zuss). We spend time with family and friends, and give presents to each other.

My name is Amir and this is my brother, Muhammed.
We live in a **Muslim** (MUZ-lim) family. *Islam* (IZ-lam) is the name of our religion.
On the map you can see the countries where most of the people are Muslim.

Our special book is called the **Qur'an** (kor-AHN).

Muslims go to a **mosque** (MAHSK)
to pray to **Allah** (ALL-ah).

Ramadan (RAH-mah-dun) is a special month of the year for Muslims. We pray and fast. Fasting means we do not eat during the day—little children are allowed to eat, though. After sunset, we eat together as a family.

Right after Ramadan comes the festival of ***Eid-al-fitr*** (EED-ul-fitter). This is one of my favourite times. We eat a special meal with our family and friends, and children get gifts.

My name is Emma and that's my sister Kayla.
In families like ours, each parent has a different religion.

My name is Connor.
My family doesn't go to a church or a mosque.

We don't practise a religion but we do believe in being kind and respectful to others.

We are Chandra and Zane, and we are **Hindu** (HIN-doo).
There are many Hindus around the world. Most of us live in **India** (IN-dee-ah).

Hindus believe in many gods and goddesses.
We go to the **_temple_** (TEM-pull) or **_mandir_** (MAN-deer) to pray.

There are many Hindu festivals during the year.

Our favourite is **Diwali** (dee-VAHL-ee), the festival of lights. We share sweets with friends and family, lighting lanterns and firecrackers to celebrate the new year.

My name is Tenzin
and I am a **Buddhist** (BOO-dist).

Buddhism (BOO-dism) is a very old religion.
Buddhists live all over the world, but mostly in Asia.

Our great teacher is **Buddha** (BOO-dah) and his teachings
are called the **Dharma** (DAR-mah).

We chant when we pray. We worship at home or at a temple.
Buddhist temples come in many shapes. This one is a **_pagoda_** (pa-GOH-dah).

Vesak (VEE-zak) or "Buddha Day" is our most important festival.
We bring flowers and light candles to celebrate Buddha's birthday.

Our names are Ben and Avah.
We are **Jewish** (JOO-ish).
Our religion is **Judaism** (JOO-day-izm).

It started a long time ago
in **Israel** (IZ-ray-ell).

Jewish families say prayers together at the **synagogue** (SIN-a-gog) or temple.

Our book of prayers is the **siddur** (SID-der).

We have lots of festivals too. **Rosh Hashanah** (rawsh hah-SHAH-nah) is the Jewish new year. We eat pieces of apple dipped in honey to wish each other a new year that is sweet and happy.

Hanukkah (HAH-nah-kah) is the festival of lights. We light the **menorah** (meh-NOR-ah), play games and give each other gifts.

The **First Peoples** of the world believe in living in harmony with nature.

My name is Michael and my family gives thanks to the **Creator** (KREE-ay-tor).

Our important teachings are told in stories and songs.

My favourite times are when we get together to sing, play drums, dance, eat, visit and tell stories.

Each of us has the right to believe or not.
As you grow up you will learn more and more about our wonderful world.

Learning about different beliefs and religions helps each of us choose what we want to believe.

Christianity

"In everything, do to others as you would have them do to you."

—*Jesus*, Matthew 7:12

Islam

"Not one of you truly believes until you wish for others what you wish for yourself."

—*The Prophet Muhammad*, Hadith

Non-Religious

"Treat others the way you want to be treated."

—The Golden Rule

Hinduism

"This is the sum of duty: do not do to others what would cause pain if done to you."

—Mahabharata 5:1517

Buddhism

"Treat not others in ways that you yourself would find hurtful."

—Udana-Varga 5.18

Judaism

"What is hateful to you, do not do to your neighbour."

—*Hillel*, Talmud, Shabbat 31a

First Peoples

"We are as much alive as we keep the earth alive."

—*Chief Dan George*

A similar code of ethics is shared by many beliefs and religions around the world.

About Judy Kirton

After careers as a primary school teacher, homemaker, and medical library technician, Judy Kirton is now retired.

"I was inspired to try writing this book by a comment made by my adult son, who said he would have liked to have known more about different religions and beliefs when he was growing up. It is my hope that the information in this little book will be well received by my grandchildren and all the children who read it."

Judy lives in Calgary, AB with Nick, her husband of 41 years, and their Sheltie, Jesse.

About Val Lawton

As a kid, Val's favourite books were the great English stories about Winnie-the-Pooh, Paddington Bear and Little Tim, as well as the tales of Roald Dahl, because the scratchy and free-wheeling illustrations left so much up to her imagination.

While Val enjoys creating art for books, she also loves working with schoolchildren as an artist-educator with the Royal Conservatory of Canada's "Learning Through the Arts" program.

Val lives in Calgary, AB with her husband, two kids and a Beagle.